T0145016

The Maker

WRITTEN BY CLARA KIM LEE
ILLUSTRATED BY BRANDON LACK

WestBow Press books may be ordered through booksellers or by contacting:

WestBow Press
A Division of Thomas Nelson & Zondervan
1663 Liberty Drive
Bloomington, IN 47403
www.westbowpress.com
1 (866) 928-1240

Because of the dynamic nature of the Internet, any web addresses or links contained in this book may have changed since publication and may no longer be valid. The views expressed in this work are solely those of the author and do not necessarily reflect the views of the publisher, and the publisher hereby disclaims any responsibility for them.

Any people depicted in stock imagery provided by Getty Images are models, and such images are being used for illustrative purposes only.
Certain stock imagery © Getty Images.

ISBN: 978-1-9736-4329-6 (sc)
ISBN: 978-1-9736-4330-2 (e)

Library of Congress Control Number: 2018912574

Print information available on the last page.

WestBow Press rev. date: 10/25/2018

WESTBOW
PRESS®
A DIVISION OF THOMAS NELSON
& ZONDERVAN

This book is dedicated to the mighty warrior and
hero of my life, Caleb Taebum Lee.

Foreword

When I started out on my journey to motherhood I had one plan: quickly get pregnant, give birth to a healthy baby, repeat every two or three years until I had three healthy children. I never imagined this journey would not take place, at least not on the easy path I had hoped and planned for. Rather, because of infertility, I found myself on a path towards adoption. And because of God's goodness and grace I found myself adopting a little girl with Down syndrome, and then two more children including a little boy with Down syndrome. And while my life has turned out to look nothing like what I had planned on all those years ago, I see now that it is better. Far better than I could have ever imagined it would be. When I coined the term, "The Lucky Few" it was because I looked around at my kids, all three adopted, two who have Down syndrome and I simply couldn't believe my luck.

What I love most about *The Maker* is there is a piece of all of our stories in it. Whether you are like me where motherhood didn't find you the way you had planned or whether you received an unexpected Down syndrome diagnosis, we can all relate to finding ourselves working on creating a life that looks far better than anything we had ever hoped for. And all of us have moments when we realize our limited understanding and scope of the world and how as a result, we can never grasp the goodness and beauty which can only be found with our Maker.

Heather Avis
Author of "The Lucky Few"

Introduction

In the summer of 2014, I flew to Cyprus for the first time for a much needed spiritual R&R. I didn't know what to expect when I signed up for a "silent retreat." We're talking about four days alone in silence, just me, my Bible and the voice of God.

Luckily, this retreat center was held in a quaint and charming village south of Nicosia. Picture narrow cobblestone walkways lined with dark wooden gates and rugged metal locks. Behind these private gates were lush gardens and blooming petals that surrounded a traditonal stone house with great big arches that were designed for the exterior and interior of the homes. It was an absolute dream to have this place to myself for four days...just me and God.

During the retreat, I took part in an art project as a way to interact with God through a creative outlet. I was instructed to roll out a large piece of paper to paint an image that I desired. The catch? I was told to paint with my non-dominant hand.

Being one that loves art and having it in my blood through creative individuals and artists like my mom and grandparents, I was looking forward to taking on this challenge! I knew exactly what I was going to paint, and I couldn't wait to get started. However, after a few short minutes into it, I was growing frustrated with the way it was turning out. What I saw in my head was not being translated onto the paper; no matter how hard I tried. I felt even more frustrated because I knew I probably couldn't have done any better with my right hand (my painting in panoramic view are on pages 18 & 26).

Relunctantly, I completed the project with dismay and remembered what I was told to do next. I stood up and walked around my painting to see if I could catch sight of something different. And as I slowly paced around my "artwork," I came to a sudden stand still as I saw something artistically beautiful and appealing to my eyes! What I saw was definitely not what I intended to paint! How could it be?! And with my left hand no less.

It was at that moment I discovered the purpose of this project and the lesson behind it.

My hope and prayer is that this personal and spiritual journey of mine will resonate with your heart as well. Whether you are a parent to a special needs child, a single seeking direction, married but at a loss for the future, etc., I hope this story will reach you and encourage you in the same way the Maker encouraged me.

Clara Kim Lee

"For my thoughts are not your thoughts, nor are your ways My ways, declares the Lord. For as the heavens are higher than the earth, so are My ways higher than your ways and My thoughts than your thoughts." Isaiah 55:8-9

My dearest baby,
Here's a picture book I want you to see.

It tells the story of a beautiful lesson we should learn,
As plans we make come with lots of twists and turns.

Let's read on to see what happens here,
You'll discover that there is nothing to fear…

I held the paintbrush in my hand,
Picturing a beautiful sunset over a vast land.

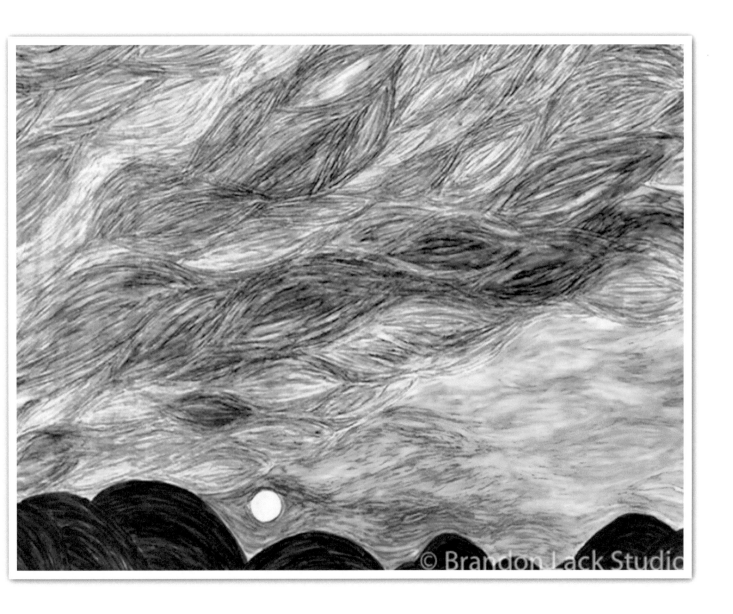

It began with strokes of yellow, orange and red,
The paintbrush dancing across the canvas as my fingers and wrist led.

It was going to be the loveliest work of art,
A creation of images painted straight from my heart.

I wanted something beautiful and perfect in every way,
Like an evening snapshot of the sun on a summer's day.

The colors I mixed together swirled two-by-two,
Creating an evening sky that began to lack a golden hue.

I added more colors here and there,
More layers to my image than I would have dared.

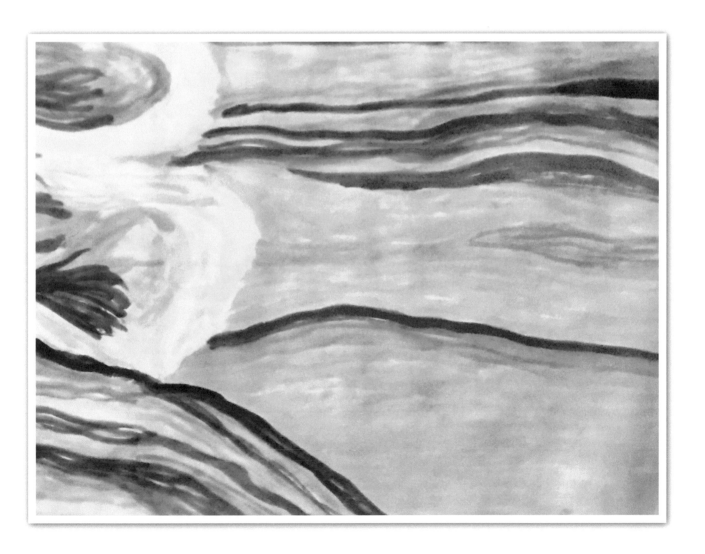

The sunset wasn't looking like the image in my head,
I wanted to give up and just go straight to bed.

As I rose from my seat and took steps to the right,
I couldn't believe what I was seeing with my eyes under the light.

My painting in this direction appeared to be something new,
It wasn't just a sunset – it was a garden too!

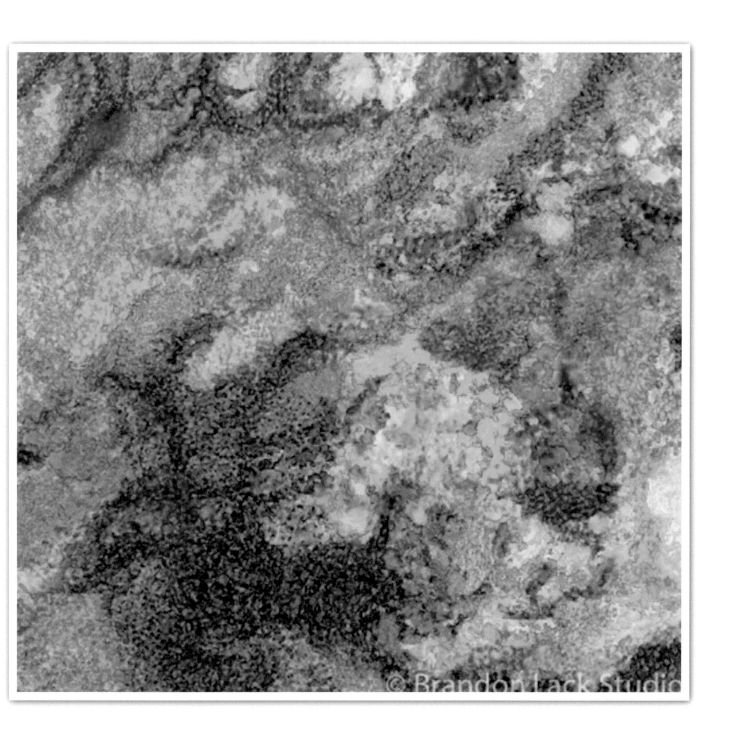

It was perfect in how it was created in every way,
I was speechless and had no words to utter or say.

I smiled with a tear in the corner of my eye,
As I looked at a garden with a flower looking up to the sky.

The blossomed yellow petals were open and stretched,
It stood tall in this garden – my heart was completely fetched.

Turn the book to the left. Do you see
a garden with a yellow flower?

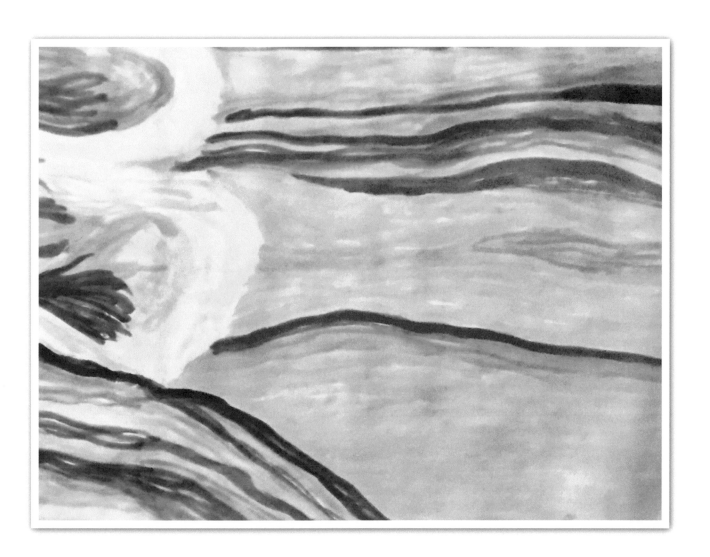

How did a painting that went all wrong,
Come out of it in the end so glorious and strong?

It was at that moment I realized the Maker behind the art,
His hands led mine all along as did His love in my heart.

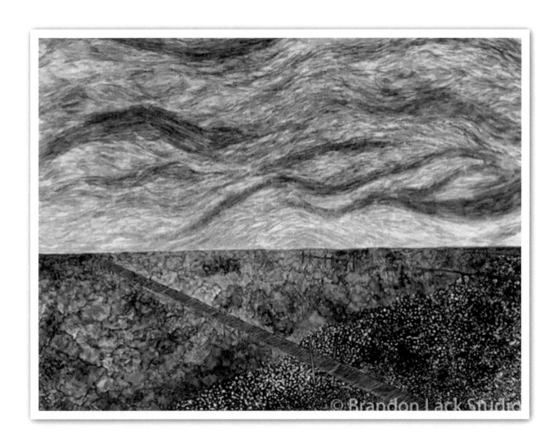

All it took was for me to see it from a different view,
To finally realize I was becoming one of "The Lucky Few."

"The Lucky Few" represents a group of parents that have something in common and that's a child with Down syndrome. It's a phrase, a mantra if you will, that was introduced by Heather Avis (speaker and author of "The Lucky Few") and now adopted by many families that have journeyed down the same bumpy, yet blessed road. We are "The Lucky Few."

About the Author

Clara K. Lee once traversed the world as a single woman, dedicating her life to full-time ministry overseas. Prior to that, she worked as an Occupational Therapist for several years. Today, she lives in Southern California with her husband and two boys. Her eldest was born prematurely at 32 weeks with Down syndrome and a rare and often fatal condition called hydrops fetalis. He spent three long months fighting for his life in NICU but has proven to be a mighty warrior ever since. Clara wrote this book as a woman of faith with a new passion and aspiration for life. She is an advocate for Down syndrome today and loves to share the beauty and blessings that come with it.

The Lee family when Clara was 36 weeks pregnant with jesse.

Brandon Lack, Artist

Brandon Lack is a handsome, happy, personable man who happens to have Down syndrome. Brandon is also an artist. His art expression process has always been connected to his challenges and his development of "self-soothing art" has not only been effective for him but inspirational for others as well.

Besides his artistic adventure, Brandon loves his family, socializing, 80's music & movies and having important things to do. He is well loved and has a relentlessly positive attitude. He lives his life with a sweetness of character and happiness that is truly profound. We believe that his innocence and kindness is expressed in his art.

Printed in the United States
By Bookmasters